PEAK OIL AND THE SECOND GREAT DEPRESSION (2010-2030)

KENNETH D. WORTH

A SURVIVAL GUIDE FOR INVESTORS
AND SAVERS AFTER PEAK OIL

PEAK OIL AND THE SECOND GREAT DEPRESSION (2010-2030)

Outskirts Press, Inc.
Denver, Colorado

Peak Oil and the Second Great Depression (2010-2030)
A Survival Guide for Investors and Savers After Peak Oil
All Rights Reserved.
Copyright © 2010 Kenneth D. Worth
v4.0

Outskirts Press, Inc.
http://www.outskirtspress.com

ISBN: 978-1-4327-6084-7

Outskirts Press and the "OP" logo are trademarks belonging to Outskirts Press, Inc.

PRINTED IN THE UNITED STATES OF AMERICA

*To my son Matthew, who when he turns 16 will ask me,
"Dad, can I have an electric car for my birthday?"*

Contents

Acknowledgements

Many individuals contributed directly or indirectly to the materials contained in this book. The author wishes to particularly thank Kenneth Deffeys, Matthew Simmons and James Puplava, whose writings on and discussions of the phenomenon of Peak Oil are essential resources in any effort to truly understand the tremendous challenge that industrial society faces in the years ahead.

Introduction

The coming two decades, 2010 to 2030, will very likely one day be known as, "The Second Great Depression." Or worse. Why am I so pessimistic? Well, two things.

The first is "Peak Oil." The second is what I refer to as Peak Debt.

Peak Oil is the point of maximum global oil production which will be followed by decade after decade of gradual production declines. Everyone accepts the fact that oil won't last forever. It is, as they say, a "finite resource." But oil in the ground is not like gas in your gas tank, which flows at a given rate and then is basically gone in the instant that you use the last drop. Rather, oil production will "Peak," i.e. reach a maximum global production rate, and then *gradually* decline as one by one the great producing oil fields that remain in the world run dry.

The actual peak will only be known conclusively in hindsight, after a decade or so of continued production declines. Initially, these production declines will be attributed to some "temporary" factor, such as the current depressed economic environment.

The facts, however, are clear. In 2005, crude oil production rose to an all-time high level of 73.8 million barrels a day (EIA, rolling 12 month average). Despite this record level of production, oil prices jumped to $40 a barrel, a price considered high at the time.

Production thereafter began slowly dropping for three years despite prices that pushed higher, to $80, and then to $100 a barrel. This rise of oil prices to unheard of levels sparked a drilling frenzy in 2005 through 2008. The net effect of all the resulting drilling, however, was only to bring production back to its former 2005 levels at about 73.8 million barrels per day. (The figures are from the Energy Information Agency, 12 month rolling averages.)

The key point is this: *much* higher prices did not lead to increased production. Rather, production plateaued in the period 2005 through 2008, despite prices that nearly quadrupled! Now, global oil production is *declining* even though prices are still more than double what they were in 2004.

In 2008, as demand continued to increase due to global economic growth while supply remained flat, prices eventually hit $148 a barrel. In the economic collapse that followed, prices dipped briefly to $40 a barrel again. However, if we smooth out the short-term fluctuation, we see that the *average* price of oil over rolling 18 month periods only rose to around $95 and has since only fallen to around $70.

Given the current economic collapse, prices should have fallen back to the $20 level. In the First Great Depression, oil prices fell to *ten cents a barrel*, or roughly $5 a barrel in today's money. Yet here we are with oil prices still above $80. Clearly, the world has changed. But how?

In the past, before Peak Oil (2005-08), as demand accelerated, Russia, Texas or Saudi Arabia could have turned on the taps to provide the extra barrels required by global consumers to keep the price from overheating with consequent negative effects on the global economy. In 2005 through 2008, however, the Saudis were powerless to restrain prices for the simple reason that they were pumping all the crude oil they could.

Texas reached maximum output way back in 1971, after which time America became increasingly dependent on imported oil. Russian production similarly peaked in 1986, after which time the Soviet Empire crumbled.

In 2008, the Saudis claimed (somewhat ridiculously) that there were "no purchasers" for their oil. All they had left to sell, however, was in fact only a million or so barrels a day of heavy sour crude filled with pollutants and very difficult to process. The light, sweet crude from the great, "super-giant" Saudi oil fields that have fueled the world for decades was being produced at maximum capacity. There simply wasn't any more to supply.

The frenzied drilling of additional wells all over the world (but especially in the Persian Gulf) only served to bring global production back up to prior levels, *not* to significantly increase it. Thereafter, as the global economy collapsed in response to the oil price shock of 2008 and the financial crisis that it helped to trigger, global production fell sharply to less than 72 million barrels per day (a decline of nearly 3% from the 12 month average). Production has since recovered in early 2010 to 73 million barrels per day, still below the 2005 highs.

Even if we do once again surpass the 74 million barrel per day level briefly, it won't really matter. Just as Texas struggled to maintain production in 1970-75, Saudi Arabia is struggling to maintain production in 2005-10. The plateau has been reached. From here, production begins falling.

On a global basis, many projects in the planning stage have now been cancelled even though prices remain high by historical standards. Exploration budgets have been slashed as major oil companies have concluded that there remains little oil left in the world to find. They are right.

What little slack now exists in the market for crude oil will be quickly gone with the next surge in demand between 2010 and 2014.

Much of what little remains to be found lies deep under the ocean floor. One of the greatest environmental disasters in history, the Gulf of Mexico Oil Spill of 2010, has now created serious doubts about our ability to recover ultra-deep water oil safely. Ask yourself. Why are we drilling miles beneath the ocean surface if we aren't running out of the stuff. Really?

Nothing explains the events of 2004 to 2010 better than the idea that we are at Peak Oil. Indeed, no other explanation really makes sense. This idea, however, is too painful for the industrial West to accept. Consequently, alternative explanations are proffered and accepted.

The most common explanation for declining global production is that production is declining because "demand has collapsed." For global consumers, however, especially those in the developing world, $85 oil is still very expensive. OPEC representatives have now stated that $85 per barrel is within the new "target price range" for crude oil.

All that is needed is global economic growth of a few percent in 2010 and the limits of OPEC production will again be tested as early as 2011. OPEC only pulled 2.75 million barrels per day of production capacity off the world market in response to the 2008-09 decline in oil prices (source: EIA).

Yet *China alone* is likely to require an additional 2.75 million barrels per day within the next *few years* as nearly a million new cars per month are sold in that country, primarily to first time buyers. Ten million new cars sold in a year means an additional million barrels per day in demand *each year* even if each new car driver only uses a few gallons of fuel a day.

The Joint Oil Data Initiative (JODI) reports that with auto sales up 70% in 2009, crude oil consumption in China increased by about 1.5 million barrels per day over 2008. There will be additional increases in 2010 and 2011.

Thus, within a few years and perhaps as early as late 2010, crude oil will be back well into triple digits and probably hitting new highs as price becomes the mechanism for rationing a limited global supply.

Peak Oil has arrived. Its primary consequence is the global economic malaise we are now experiencing. Any return to global economic growth will cause oil prices to spike up again causing the recovery to falter. This means that continued economic growth in China (currently at a 9% annual rate) or anywhere else in the developing world will cause continued economic contraction in the more developed economies.

To make matters worse, Peak Oil has hit the developed economies at a time when they are least prepared for it. Americans especially have piled up trillions of dollars of debt of all kinds, most especially mortgage debt as a result of the real estate bubble. The federal government is now adding 1.5 trillion dollars in debt per year to what is already a tremendous debt burden.

After the First Great Depression, Americans avoided debt if at all possible. The crushing effects of debt in a prolonged economic downturn had just been demonstrated unforgettably as a third of homeowners with a mortgage lost their homes. By 2007, however, all the lessons of the First Great Depression had apparently been forgotten, and debt of all kinds rose to levels never before seen in American history.

Homeowner percent equity which had been above 80% in the early 1950's fell to around 40%. Mortgage debt as a percent of GDP rose from around 15% in the 1950's to 75% today. Currently, in early 2010, while mortgage debt outstanding is declining as homes are lost to foreclosure, runaway government borrowing has increased total debt levels in society to an unprecedented three times annual disposable income (Sources: Federal Reserve, Bureau of Economic Analysis)

Peak Oil alone presents tremendous challenges. Together with Peak Debt, the results will likely be calamitous. Time will tell if the 73.8 million barrel per day level will ever again be breached. If it is surpassed, it will only be briefly in 2010-11.

If we conclude that Peak Oil is now in fact past, or close to it, certain things follow for investors, savers and those with a taste for speculation.

In the chapters that follow, I make a more detailed argument regarding why 2005-08 was most likely Peak Oil. I also look at the probable consequences of Peak Oil and Peak Debt for the American economy and for the investing public. This will involve looking at which sectors of the economy to avoid as investors and which to favor. I also examine allocation between asset classes as well as consider of the role of commodities in a Peak Oil Portfolio. I also evaluate at cash and cash equivalents, the traditional stores of value.

Ultimately, the purpose of this book is to give you the information you need, as well as an easy to follow game plan to successfully navigate the coming Great Oil Crisis and the consequent Second Great Depression.

There are no guarantees, just a simple proposal for surviving in a post-Peak world.

Part One:
Peak Oil and the Second Great Depression

CHAPTER **1**

What Is "Peak Oil?"

Oil is not going to just "run out." Rather, production will stagnate and then begin to fall as the largest and most productive oil fields remaining in the world slowly run dry.

Crude oil production in the United States increased gradually from its discovery in the 1860's to around 10 million barrels a day around 1970. US production thereafter declined from 10 million barrels per day to around 5 million barrels per day in 2009. US oil production thus "peaked" around 1970.

Dramatic improvements in oil field technology and sharp increases in the oil price during the 1970's could not stop this decline. America's crude oil resource was simply being depleted and eventually, by 2050, it will essentially be gone.

The idea that productive fields are being kept from oil producers by needless environmental protections is a complete myth. Oil and natural gas production is ongoing even in our *National Parks and Seashores* including Padre Island National Seashore in Texas.

The only *significant* quantity of oil currently protected from production is the Alaskan National Wildlife Refuge (ANWR). From a global supply perspective, what limited oil might exist in that frozen wasteland is completely irrelevant, totaling maybe a month of global consumption.

Unfortunately, the fact is that global oil production is peaking today and will decline from around 74 million barrels per day in 2008, to about 35 million barrels per day in 2050.

Peak Oil is the point of maximum global production. We are now at that point.

CHAPTER 2

The Saudi Peak = the Global Peak

The big Saudi oil fields that have served as the world's spare capacity since the oil shocks of the 1970's are now rolling over and going into decline. The fact that they lasted this long, having been discovered in the 1940's and 1950's and developed soon thereafter, was only due to production restrictions placed on them first by Western oilmen and then by Saudi rulers.

The Saudi Arabian Peninsula was fully explored by Saudi Aramco (a consortium of American companies) between the end of World War II and 1979, when the Saudis took back control of their oil fields. The total original recoverable resource was estimated in 1979 at about 150 billion barrels, with remaining reserves of about 100 billion barrels. Up until 1979, Saudi Arabia had produced "only" 50 billion barrels of oil.

Private oil companies, however, tend to understate reserves somewhat. When the Saudis took control their oil fields in 1979, they revised their reserve estimates to about 150 billion barrels and upped their estimates of the original recoverable resource to 200 billion barrels. These numbers are probably very close to being accurate.

Saudi Arabia has now produced around 120 billion barrels of oil, or 60% of its original recoverable resource. Current reserves left in the ground are probably around 80 billion barrels.

After the collapse of oil prices in 1986, OPEC nations began inflating their claimed reserves to get around the quotas they themselves had established. In 1988, Saudi Arabia's claimed reserves, which had been creeping upward, went from 169.6 billion barrels to 255 billion barrels despite the fact that no major discovery was made that year. Indeed, the Saudi Arabian peninsula had already been exhaustively explored in the period between 1930 and 1970.

All the major Saudi fields currently being produced were found during that time. In fact, the vast majority of Saudi oil comes from just seven enormous, "super-giant" fields.

Saudi oil ministers have since continued to increase their reserves figure to the current ridiculous number of 276 billion barrels despite annual production of around three billion barrels and cumulative production of 120 billion barrels out of the original 200 billion.

In all likelihood, 200 billion barrels is all the oil we will ever get out of Saudi Arabia. The Saudi mega-fields have now pumped about 120 billion barrels (according to established sources of production statistics). Sure, there are probably some 80 billion barrels left under the Saudi desert. Maybe there are 100 billion barrels. We can only hope. But the world uses about 25 billion barrels of oil a year.

When an oil region reaches the point at which half of its recoverable resource has been extracted, production typically begins to decline. This has proven true for every major oil region in the world including Texas and West Siberia. It will prove true for Saudi Arabia as well.

It may be that advanced drilling techniques such as horizontal "maximum reservoir contact" wells have extended the Saudi peak somewhat to the 60% mark and the present day. But this has merely delayed the decline and will make it more precipitous now that it has arrived.

The basic idea is this: if you drill wells horizontally through an oil reservoir rather than vertically, you can maintain flow rates as a field matures because most of the well remains in contact with the remaining oil. But when the water column used to push the oil to the surface hits the horizontal wells, oil production collapses rather than declines gradually as it would with a vertical well.

Thus, the peak of production from a given field such as Saudi Arabia's Ghawar can be delayed by drilling horizontally, but the decline in production will be much more dramatic when it finally arrives. For a more technical discussion of this subject please consult the writings of Princeton University geologist Kenneth Deffeys, including *Hubbert's Peak* and *Beyond Oil*.

A collapse of production in just one of Saudi Arabia's seven major oil fields would be a major blow to global oil supply. A collapse of production in Ghawar would be catastrophic. It will happen eventually. The only question is when.

When Saudi Arabia enters production decline, the world will have entered production decline as well, as there are no countries with increasing production large enough to offset declining production in Saudi Arabia, together with the continued declines in other producing countries such as the US. *All* scenarios of rising global production in the years ahead rely heavily on significant Saudi crude oil production increases. These will not be forthcoming.

The production details of Saudi oil fields are shrouded in secrecy. Saudi oil ministers say they can increase production. The problem is that when push came to shove, the Saudis could not hold oil below $100. Rather, the oil price spiked to $148 and a global economic meltdown ensued.

The fact is that by their actions, Saudi oil ministers have proven that their fields have peaked and that production is now about to decline. For several years now, Saudi Arabia has been engaged in infill drilling in its major fields to try to maintain current levels of production. More and more wells drilled in the same reservoir in order to produce the same amount of oil is a sure sign that production is about to begin to decline significantly.

This is precisely what happened in Texas and other major producing regions after they peaked. If there were 276 billion barrels of oil still in the ground, it would not take the drilling of more and more wells into the same seven reservoirs to maintain production at prior levels. Rather, additional drilling should be resulting in increased production and it has not.

Saudi Arabian officials claim that new projects including development of the Khurais field have added 1.8 million barrels per day of additional capacity to meet future demand. Maybe this is true. And maybe production in other fields will not decline sufficiently to offset this new production. Ultimately, it just doesn't matter. China alone increased consumption by 1.5 million barrels per day in 2009.

In all likelihood, as demand recovers in 2010 to 2014, especially demand from China and the rest of the developing world, the Saudis will be powerless to restrain prices which will surge to $200 a barrel.

What will come next will be a seemingly never-ending Great Oil Crisis.

CHAPTER 3

The Consequences of Peak Oil

If we are lucky, global oil production after Peak Oil will decline at a gradual annual rate, around 2% per year. After the US passed its peak oil production in 1971 (when the Texas oil fields reached peak production), US production began a slow decline over the following 39 years that continues to this day. Even the addition of mega-fields like Prudhoe Bay in Alaska, the largest field ever discovered in North America, did not prevent the overall, gradual 2% annual decline.

The discovery of another mega-field like Saudi Arabia's Ghawar in some forgotten corner of the world is a very unlikely possibility at this point in time. Say another Ghawar were discovered tomorrow. This would do nothing to prevent the global production declines that are coming.

The coming decline in production is about 35 million barrels per day over 40 years. Production will decline from around 74 million barrels per day today to around 39 million barrels per day in 2050. Yet Ghawar at its most prolific only produced about 5 million barrels per day.

Five million barrels per day is an extraordinary quantity of oil for an entire nation let alone from a single field. Yet this is less than 7% of current demand.

What is needed is not just another Ghawar, but another entire Persian Gulf. But where will we find it? The last great oil discoveries were in 1968 and 1976 when we found the Alaska North Slope and then Mexico's Cantarell field. Since then, not a single super-giant field has been found, let alone a new producing region.

Where is there left to look? Antarctica? Good luck with that!

Peak US production in 1971 was approximately 10 million barrels per day. Most people don't realize it, but the US once was the Saudi Arabia of oil with about 250 billion barrels of recoverable resource and maximum sustained output of around 10 million barrels per day. Our giant fields, however, were found much earlier, and pumped dry sooner.

Once the US passed peak, American production declined steadily at about 2% per year. The cumulative effect of those 2% cumulative declines is the current level of US production at approximately 5 million barrels a day, an overall decline of about 50% in just under 40 years.

The production profile of the entire globe will parallel that of individual large producing regions, just as the profile of large producing regions parallels that of individual fields.

Production increases steadily until approximately 50% of the resource has been extracted, then it crests and gradually declines. Please consult the writings of Kenneth Deffeys for more details regarding precisely why this is so. Interestingly enough, production profiles follow a bell-shaped curve (technically, a logistic curve) that allows a prediction of the timing of the peak, well in advance.

M. King Hubbert, who was a geologist with Shell Oil Co. at the time, predicted in the 1950's that based on mathematical models of production, American oil supply would peak around 1965-70 and that global oil production would peak in approximately the year 2005. He turns out to have been very close with regard to American production which peaked in 1971 and very close to the actual date for the global peak as well, which was very likely in 2005-08.

In the 1970's, once America's swing producer, Texas, went into decline, the US necessarily went into decline as well despite the discovery of mega-fields such as Prudhoe Bay in Alaska. Similarly, with Saudi Arabia in decline, global production will continue to decline despite increased production from Africa and other emerging nations.

Tar sands, and extra-heavy oil even under the rosiest scenarios cannot offset 2% annual declines in conventional petroleum production as these are at best expected to contribute a small fraction of what will be lost as Saudi Arabia's and other nations' conventional production falls.

Alternative liquids such as biodiesel and ethanol will moderate the decline to some degree, just as the addition of the Alaska North Slope moderated the American decline, but overall we will be looking at 2% declines per year, year after year, until we transition to an alternative transportation fuel.

This will most likely be nuclear generated electricity stored in batteries, supplemented by small combustion engines that are used only for longer trips, (i.e. plug-in hybrids).

Replacing the entire transportation refueling infrastructure with natural gas or hydrogen refilling stations will likely be too expensive to be practical. By contrast, the transition to plug-in hybrids can be seamless; indeed, the infrastructure already exists.

The coming declines in global crude oil production will be largely price-insensitive. US production declined from 1971 onward despite the fact that oil prices rose from a few dollars a barrel in 1971, to 40 dollars a barrel during the Iran-Iraq War in 1982. The fact that prices were 20 times higher in the early 1980's was insufficient to raise American production above the 1971 levels because the great producing fields of Texas were slowly beginning to run dry. Higher prices couldn't stop that. Neither did the presence of extra-heavy oil or oil shale.

This will be the case for the global decline as well. High prices will be unable to stem the global production decline once the great Saudi mega-fields have themselves gone into decline. Prices will rise to levels that will force the necessary reductions in consumption, given the fact that no more oil will be available.

Just as higher prices for whale oil (used for indoor lighting) did not put more whales into the ocean in the late 19th Century, higher prices for crude oil will not put more of that limited resource in the ground, recoverable at prices consumers can afford. Indeed, it was the high price of whale oil that led to the development of "rock oil," i.e. petroleum. Gradually, kerosene derived from crude oil replaced whale oil for indoor lighting which was the single largest application for crude oil prior to the popularization of the automobile in the 1920's.

Unfortunately, most consumers in the developed world are themselves largely price insensitive when it comes to oil. Thus, it will take sustained, *very* high prices to force consumers to buy small, hybrid vehicles in large quantities, use mass transit and restrict driving. This is because for most people in the US, liquid fuel consumption for transportation represents just a few thousand dollars a year in expenditures.

A driver who travels a typical 1200 miles per month and gets a fairly typical 20 miles per gallon, only uses 60 gallons of gasoline per month. At $3.00 per gallon that is $180 per month. A rise in the price of gasoline to even $6.00 a gallon only costs the typical driver an extra $180 per month. This is unlikely to force major lifestyle changes for a typical American worker who takes home about $2,500 per month.

On the other hand, a driver trading a Suburban for a Prius can cut his or her fuel consumption by more than 50%. Since we only need to reduce global consumption by 2-3% per year, most of the gains will come from lifestyle changes of those with the lowest incomes and the longest commutes, as well as people of modest means currently driving the largest, most fuel-inefficient vehicles.

To some extent, we got a glimpse of the future in response to the 2008 oil price shocks. Going forward, the point of capitulation to higher prices will slowly move its way up the income scale, to those with more moderate commutes and to vehicles currently viewed as relatively more efficient such as medium-sized SUV's and large sedans.

What complicates the prospect of global reductions in fuel consumption is the emergence of the developing world, and China and India in particular. A million new cars a month are being sold to Chinese consumers. I'll repeat that last point, **a million new cars a month are being sold to Chinese consumers**. Sales in 2009 *increased* 70% compared to the prior year despite the global economic downturn.

Most of these sales are additions to the global vehicle fleet as older models are sold to other consumers rather than being retired from use. Many new car sales in China are to first-time buyers.

The global economy needs to reduce total consumption by 2-3% per year going forward. Cash-rich Chinese and Indians are unlikely to refrain from purchasing and driving automobiles just so cash-strapped Americans can continue to drive inefficient SUV's.

As a result, we can expect that increases in oil imports by China and India will continue to come at the expense of America, and to a lesser extent, Europe and Japan. Americans consume roughly twice as much oil per capita compared to Europeans and Japanese. Consequently, Americans will be forced by high prices to make relatively greater modifications to their behavior. To some extent, Japanese and Europeans will be insulated from the worst effects of Peak Oil by the burdensome taxes that already make petroleum products so expensive in those economies.

There is no sense, however, "blaming" the developing world for increasing demand and driving up oil prices. For over 100 years, economic growth has required higher and higher volumes of crude oil. Up until 2005-2008, increased supply was always available to meet the increased demand, although in the 1970's and early 80's that increased supply was offered at a high price.

After Peak Oil, i.e. after 2005-08, there just won't be any additional supply. Pundits tell us that the problem is one of increased demand from China and India. That is precisely wrong. The problem is supply that has plateaued and is now falling.

Global demand is actually shrinking in response to high prices. 2010 production will be *below* that of 2005, five years earlier. Increased demand never was a problem before. Why should it be a problem now?

Historically, oil production (both supply and demand) increased approximately 7% per year up until the oil shocks of the 1970's as automobiles and trucking became widespread in the West. Thereafter, oil production grew at a slower 2% annual rate as electric power generation and other industrial applications were switched away from oil to coal and natural gas due to high crude oil prices.

This slowing of production growth between 1980 and 2005 is entirely consistent with M. King Hubbert's prediction of a "bellshaped" curve of oil production on a global basis with a peak around the year 2005.

Now, the global economy wants to continue to grow and to consume more oil. The problem is that oil production is falling and will continue to do so. No additional oil will be available at *any* price.

To make matters even worse for the developed nations, oil exporting nations, including Russia and Saudi Arabia, can be expected to increase consumption rather than reduce it in response to higher oil prices. Higher oil prices will increase living standards in these countries and higher living standards will result in increases in fuel consumption rather than decreases even as oil prices rise dramatically. Indeed, OPEC oil consumption has continued to rise in 2007, 2008 and 2009, even as Western oil consumption has fallen dramatically in response to high prices and the global economic contraction.

Fuel prices in many oil exporting nations are subsidized and will not reflect the global price increases. Net exports from these nations will decline dramatically as production falls and domestic consumption increases.

Thus, the price of oil will need to rise to the point where US consumers reduce consumption by roughly 3-4% a year, year after year after year after year. In other words, the price of oil will rise to a painful level and then continue to climb, in real terms, for decades. The rise will not be linear, as oil price shocks tend to have disruptive effects on the economy, and a contracting economy tends to result in lower oil prices.

We saw this in 2008-09, as a contracting global economy caused oil prices to fall from near $150 a barrel to around $40 a barrel. Of course, just a few years ago, $40 a barrel was considered a *very* high price for oil. When the global economy recovers in the years ahead, the price of oil will surge to a new high, in the $200 a barrel range. This will cause another contraction in the global economy and another "crash" in oil prices, but very likely only down to around $100.

This cycle will likely be repeated many times in the coming decades.

Prices won't go to infinity, of course. Very high, *painful*, prices will force changes in behavior with a lag, as consumers trading in vehicles opt for more fuel-efficient ones, with high-mileage and lower-income drivers taking the lead. Painfully high levels of unemployment will reduce commuting and limit recreational driving.

Ultimately, prices only need to remain high enough to force continued 2-3% reductions in global consumption. From a long-term perspective, we need to reduce global crude oil consumption by 50% over a period of some 40 years. That is a long time to get the world's drivers into plug-in hybrids, electrified railway and other forms of transportation that use less petroleum than the typical 2010 automobile.

Similarly, rail and ocean transport will gradually replace trucking for transportation of goods. Rail transport is five times more efficient than highway trucking. Ocean transport is 20 times more efficient.

This process won't be the end of the world. But it will sure feel like it to US consumers!

CHAPTER 4

The Economic Effects of $300 Oil

Three hundred dollar oil in today's money translates into a price at the pump of roughly $8.00. That will force a lot of change for American households. If you think that $300 oil is unlikely, just remember that the last oil shocks in the 1970's and early 80's saw the price of oil rise 20-fold from around $2 a barrel to $40 a barrel.

A mere 15-fold increase in oil price in real terms from $20 (1990's) to $300 (2010's), in response to Peak Oil is probably a best-case scenario. With inflation of all prices, the nominal price of oil could go significantly higher, to $500, or $1,000 per barrel.

Since many consumers are price insensitive when it comes to oil, it will likely take at least $8.00 gasoline (in 2010 dollars) rather than $6 or $7 gasoline to force the necessary behavioral changes on a large enough scale.

The price rise is not likely to happen all at once. There will be price spikes followed by modest declines to "new normal" levels. Over the decade 2010 to 2020, however, we can expect an overall increase in prices to the $300 level (in 2010 dollars), followed by a period of 'adjustment' as consumers transition to lower levels of consumption via the purchase of more fuel-efficient cars, moving closer to work or utilizing public transit. Many Americans will be out of work and will not need to commute at all.

What $300 oil (in 2010 dollars) mostly will accomplish, however, is a massive transfer of wealth from the US, Europe, China and Japan to the oil exporting countries. The US imports about 13 million barrels of oil a day. At a price of $300 a barrel, that represents about 1.4 trillion dollars a year. That's about $15,000 per household per year! But Americans only earn about $60,000 a year. Clearly, something has to give.

Half of American oil consumption is in the form of gasoline and diesel for personal transportation. The rest is comprised largely of trucking fuel, airplane jet fuel and bunker fuel for ocean transport. Clearly, $8.00 gasoline will force many people into smaller cars and will reduce a great deal of inessential driving.

However, many individuals will just grin and bear it, as many did after the oil shocks of the 70's and early 80's. Those wishing to drive 20 mpg vehicles 1200 miles per month will have to pay $480 per month or $5,760 per year! Those forking over nearly $6,000 a year at the pump, will have little choice but to cut back elsewhere. This will crush the domestic economy.

The burden of high oil prices will fall disproportionately on the less well-off. About half of American workers take home somewhere between $1,000 and $2,000 per month. For those relying on say $1,500 a month, an increase in fuel costs of $200 per month results in a 13% loss of disposable income. That is money that is already going to rent, food and clothing.

Many Americans are already out of work. Official unemployment figures are around 9%. However, this number excludes anyone who hasn't looked for work in the last week, anyone who hasn't worked in over a year, and anyone working only part-time who would like a full-time job if one were available. The real unemployment number is already closer to 20%.

When the next oil price shock comes in a few years, unemployment will surge to levels not seen since the First Great Depression. Gradually, and not too long from now, we will begin to realize that the Second Great Depression is already well underway.

Overall, as a result of high levels of unemployment and with tremendous efforts in conservation, American oil consumption might be reduced to 15 million barrels per day from the current 19 (already down from 21 as a result of the economic contraction.) With domestic production of 5 million bpd remaining, this still leaves imports of 10 million bpd. Yet at $300 per barrel, the outflow of dollars will still reach 1.1 trillion a year.

The larger economic effects of an outflow of 1.1 trillion dollars a year will naturally be very significant, even for an economy as large as that of the US.

In the past, Americans have financed their trade deficit (including the deficit in oil) by borrowing from abroad. Now, however, Americans (at least those other than the government itself) are carrying too much debt to borrow further to purchase expensive foreign oil.

The Federal government has emerged as "borrower and spender of last resort." However, it is unlikely that the oil-exporting nations will have a limitless appetite for Treasury securities. At some point, the US government will reach the limits of its ability to borrow. Given the current rate of borrowing (deficits of well over a trillion dollars a year), together with the current federal debt that is now over 13 trillion dollars, that point is not likely to be very far off, say 2015.

This 13 trillion dollar figure, an astonishing $130,000 per American household, includes the debt to the Social Security and Medicare Trust Funds which is currently over four trillion dollars. This obligation to future Social Security and Medicare recipients represents a legitimate debt of the Treasury that will have to be repaid at least in significant part.

The end of foreign borrowing together with $300 oil will force the "downsizing" of America. The US dollar will need to fall relative to other currencies to a point where imports more or less equal exports. Needless to say, the dollar will need to fall a great deal if we are importing a trillion dollars worth of oil a year, in addition to everything else we import.

A trillion dollars for imported oil each year will mean less money for the domestic economy which will necessarily shrink. Faced with levels of unemployment not seen since the First Great Depression, the Nation will call out for something or someone to end the economic misery.

CHAPTER 5

"Peak Debt" and the Coming Hyperinflation

The Federal Reserve has a dual mandate, to promote price stability and full employment. With domestic spending reduced by the massive outflow of dollars due to high priced fuel, unemployment will be intolerably high, and the Fed will be forced to increase the money supply sufficiently to create inflation to stimulate the economy. Fed Governors who refuse to assist the American people in this regard will simply be replaced.

Inflation will actually help the majority of Americans who are currently buried in mortgage debt. As wages rise, mortgages (which in most cases are fixed for 30 years) will be less burdensome on homeowners. This will free up money for spending in the domestic economy and reduce unemployment.

Given the current debt levels borne by households, $8.00 gasoline (largely imported from abroad) virtually guarantees the arrival of the Second Great Depression. In order to prevent economic catastrophe, the Fed will have no practical alternative to increasing the price level by 200 percent or more. This can be accomplished by a decade of 12% inflation.

Already, in response to the financial crisis of 2007-08, the

Fed has almost tripled its "balance sheet" from about 800 billion dollars to 2.3 trillion dollars. For reasons discussed below, these actions have not yet produced significant inflation. Ultimately, however, continued monetization of ongoing Federal deficits (i.e. printing of money that is then lent to the Treasury Department) will produce the desired inflation.

It may be that the money printing that has already occurred is sufficient to create significant inflation once private lending returns to normal. In any case, inflation is on its way.

Overall, the price level will very likely rise at least 5 fold over the coming two decades as Peak Oil and Peak Debt combine with structural problems in the US federal budget related to Social Security and Medicare, universal health care and an overstretched US military.

It's not like we don't all see it coming.

When the Fed wishes to increase the money supply and create inflation, it buys something in the "open market," i.e. from an ordinary person like you or me, or perhaps your banker. Usually, this is a Treasury security, like a Treasury bond or note, that then appears on the Fed's "balance sheet" as an asset. The Fed then credits the purchase price in the account of the member bank of the seller. This credit is new money that is created out of thin air.

When the Fed buys a trillion dollars worth of stuff, whether it is Treasury bonds, securities backed by subprime mortgages or beanie babies, it is creating a lot of fresh money in the bank accounts of the lucky sellers. Ultimately, this money will find its way into the real economy, driving up prices, and more importantly, wages.

The primary seller of these assets will be the Federal Government itself as it issues trillions of dollars worth of bonds and notes to fund its profligate spending. This money can then be distributed to ordinary citizens via programs such as home purchase tax credits, "cash for clunkers," extended unemployment benefits, and so on. The idea is simply to get money into the hands of people to stimulate spending and, ultimately, to raise the price level.

Together with price increases due to oil shocks and the decline of the US dollar, the stage has been set for a true Hyperinflation.

The value to you of a piece of paper with a picture of George Washington on in is that someone else will take that piece of paper in exchange for something you might want or need. The relative value of coffee cups, shares of Google stock or plane tickets to Hawaii is constantly changing depending on supply and demand. The same is true for pictures of George Washington in relation to everything else.

To understand how inflation is created, consider the following hypothetical example. Let's say the Federal Reserve offers you ten trillion dollars for your most prized beanie baby. Since the relative value to you of the ten trillion dollars very likely exceeds that of even your most prized beanie baby, you accept. This is an "open market transaction" in which the Fed has purchased an asset (which will appear on its "balance sheet") for newly printed cash.

At this point, however, the general price level is unaffected. You may be the type of person who only wishes to store your ten trillion in a warehouse somewhere and just think about it being there. If you are, the price level in the economy will remain unchanged.

Printing money is not enough to cause inflation. The money that is printed must move through the economy to affect prices. Economists call this movement the "velocity" of money. The faster the money moves, the more inflation is created by a given amount of money printing.

Let's say you are like most of us and the idea of your ten trillion dollars just gathering dust in a warehouse somewhere is not particularly appealing to you. Rather, the relative value to you of all the things for which you might exchange at least some of those pictures of George Washington greatly exceeds the value to you of the pictures themselves.

Indeed, by exchanging ten trillion dollars for your beanie baby, the Fed has dramatically altered the value to you of a picture of

George Washington relative to everything else. Previously, you might have had to work pretty hard to get just a thousand of those pictures. Now, well, you could burn a ten billion of them and have your wealth essentially unaffected.

Consequently, you spend.

When you go into the marketplace, however, to exchange your pictures of George Washington for goods and services, you will find the price level largely the same as it was before you sold your most prized beanie baby to the Fed. That is, prices in the marketplace do not yet reflect the fact that a fresh ten trillion dollars have just been created.

This is a tremendous benefit to you as you are able to purchase goods and services, at least initially, at today's low prices.

Previously, there were many things you wanted but did not purchase as the relative value to you of a picture of George Washington was fairly high in relation to them (perhaps because you did not have that many pictures of G.W. in your possession.) Now, however, since you can spend ten billion pictures of old George and remain in essentially the same financial condition you are in currently, you find yourself willing to purchase all sorts of things.

With great effort, let's say you spend a hundred million dollars. You buy mansions, cars, vacations to wherever you previously wanted to go; you buy gifts for anyone and everyone you can think of, Babe Ruth autograph baseballs, whatever. You probably overpay for much of it, but you don't care, as those pictures of George Washington still don't have very much value to you relative to the goods and services that you can get with them.

Because you were the first recipient of the new money printed by the Fed when it gave you ten trillion dollars for your beanie baby, you were the greatest beneficiary of that transaction. You were able to go out into the marketplace and purchase at the then current prices. This demonstrates one of the basic principles of the impact of inflation, that the individuals and entities (including governmental entities) that first receive the newly printed money are the ones who benefit the most.

In our example, that is you. In the real world today, it is the big banks and Wall Street firms that got to unload their own "beanie babies," i.e. their mortgage-backed securities and other toxic waste to the Fed for 1.5 trillion pictures of George Washington.

To return to our hypothetical example, you have thus far spent a hundred million dollars. Yet, you still have 9.9999 trillion dollars. Clearly, you need to keep spending.

Now, your Aunt Betty is currently living on what she earns as a stocker at Wal-Mart which isn't very much. The value to her of a picture of George Washington relative to everything else is pretty high. Let's say you give Aunt Betty ten million dollars for the '63 Corvette of hers that you always wanted to drive.

Since you were kind enough to give her ten million pictures of George Washington for her classic American car, she will find the relative value of each of those pictures compared to the goods and services in the marketplace dramatically altered. Just as you began spending your ten trillion, she will perhaps begin spending her ten million.

In this way, each person with whom you transact as you try to spend your funds will find his or her own preferences regarding the relative value of pictures of George Washington and everything else altered.

Aunt Betty previously placed such a high value on a picture of George Washington that she was willing to stock shelves at Walmart for an entire hour in exchange for just ten of them. Now, her preferences have changed and the value to her of an hour of time is far greater than just ten dollars. She quits her job, buys a new house and starts gardening. Aunt Betty is also a beneficiary of the ten trillion dollars you received for your beanie baby.

As your cash begins to move through the economy, individuals will find that they can raise the prices that they ask for goods and services. Indeed, they find that as the relative value to them of the pictures of George Washington falls, they are most unwilling to part with their goods and services at the old prices, just as Aunt Betty is no longer willing to work for $10 per hour.

It should seem obvious, of course, that the Fed can't make us all rich by buying our trifles with newly printed money. Indeed, it can't. For every person who gains from inflation, such as you in our example, there is someone else who loses.

Let's say that when you were spending your first 100 million dollars, you bought a nice-sized ranch in Montana. You always did want to be a rancher, after all. Let's say you paid ten million dollars for it. Now the seller of this ranch was a man named Wilson. He was getting older and didn't have any children to take it over. He gladly accepted the ten million pictures of George Washington you offered him in exchange for his 10,000 or so acres.

Mr. Wilson didn't trust the stock market and wanted to make sure he had funds for his old age, so he put the ten million dollars in three month Treasury bills earning .16% per year. There it sits.

Eventually, you realize that you can't possibly spend ten trillion dollars, so you just start giving the money away. You give money to all your friends, just for liking you. You give money to anyone who buys a home, is unemployed, installs solar panels or just buys a more efficient car. You are a generous person.

Gradually, the ten trillion dollars that the Fed gave you for your beanie baby works its way through society, transforming the relative value of goods and services and pictures of George Washington, just as it did with you and Aunt Betty.

Eventually, the price level rises dramatically. I'm not sure how much the price level would rise from the transaction we are considering, but let's say it rises ten-fold. The ranch you bought for ten million dollars is now worth 100 million dollars. Mr. Wilson, however, finds that the Treasury bills he is holding are still only worth 10 million dollars and that the value of that 10 million dollars in terms of the goods and services that individuals are willing to exchange for them has dropped dramatically.

He has ten million dollars, but a gallon of gas is $30, a haircut costs $140, and the median family income is $600,000. His old ranch now is valued at 100 million dollars, and he could never buy it back. In terms of purchasing power, Mr. Wilson has lost 90% of his wealth.

Thus, in our scenario, you and your Aunt Betty benefitted while Mr. Wilson (and anyone else holding cash or its near equivalent) lost out. Indeed, since printing pieces of paper cannot produce real wealth for society, your gain was roughly equivalent to the losses experienced by Mr. Wilson and others like him who were holding cash.

In the real world, thusfar, the shareholders and bondholders of the big banks and Wall Street firms, many of whom now control the Treasury department itself, have benefitted. If their companies hadn't gotten a trillion dollars for their various "beanie babies," most would have seen their investments in those companies wiped out.

Who lost? Anyone who had cash or cash equivalents which would have risen in value in a deflationary environment has lost. Anyone earning .01% interest in a bank account while inflation averages 5% has lost.

In other words, the insiders on Wall Street won. The average American lost. No surprise there. It's just business as usual in Washington. As a consolation prize, to the extent your 401(k) has some big bank stock or bonds in it, you benefited too. Wahoo!

Inflation clearly benefits those with first access to the newly printed money who can transact at the old prices. It also significantly acts to transfer wealth from creditors to debtors as the real value of money declines.

Mr. Wilson loaned ten million dollars to the US government when he purchased that quantity of Treasury bills. In exchange, he was promised .16% interest (or $16,000 per year) and the eventual return of his money. After the real value of money declined by a factor of ten, the government found that it did not owe

Mr. Wilson nearly so much in as it had before compared to the taxes it collected from the average American household, which now earns $600,000 per year. Likewise, Mr. Wilson found that his claim on the government was dramatically reduced in terms of the real purchasing power of the money he was owed.

Given the fact that the US Federal government is the world's largest individual debtor, now owing around 13 trillion dollars, the Fed will inflate with implicit support from the President and Congress. (By the time this book reaches you hands, the national debt, which is increasing by around 1.5 trillion dollars per year, will likely be much higher. You can check the current national debt at www.usdebtclock.org.)

The Federal debt is now nearly 100% of GDP and seems headed for 200% within the decade. Realistically, the only way to get out of a debt larger than 100% of GDP (apart from printing money) is spending cuts and higher taxes, together with strong growth in the economy. American lawmakers, however, currently seem to have no taste for spending cuts or *significant* tax increases, and Peak Oil will crush the economy in the years ahead, preventing growth for decades. Thus, the only way out will be to print away the debt burden.

If prices rise significantly, GDP will rise as well, though only in paper terms. But if the national debt is denominated in paper dollars, the level of the debt to GDP can shrink dramatically simply by the Fed printing money. This it will need to do.

Most Americans own the home they now live in. By the time real estate prices stop their current decline, somewhere around 2011, the mirage of wealth that was the real estate bubble will be gone, but a massive debt load will remain for most households. Inflation, especially wage inflation, will be welcomed as reducing the real burden of this debt. If wages can rise by even a factor of two, the burden of home mortgages on most households can be dramatically reduced.

Since much of America's debt is held by China (two trillion dollars), Japan (one trillion dollars), and the oil exporting nations (two trillion dollars), the effect of inflation will be to relieve Americans of much of their financial obligations to the rest of the world. This will be necessary as Americans will be struggling under the financial pressure of $8.00 gasoline.

In addition, much of the rest of the nation's debt is held by America's well-to-do, including many multi-millionaires and billionaires, who have prospered over the past 25 years as financial assets and the profits of businesses using outsourced labor have soared in value while the real wages of American workers have stagnated. The expropriation of the fixed-income assets (as well as the bank deposits) of these individuals via inflation will be accepted as politically necessary given the dire circumstances in which the Nation will find itself.

Inflation will be a useful tool for policy makers in the coming difficulties. It cannot, however, solve all the problems faced by the oil consuming nations. Ultimately, even though the debt burden will be effectively removed, in essence a bankruptcy filing by the American people, there will be the continuing problem of financing a 15 million barrel per day consumption habit.

Filing for bankruptcy just eliminates your debts. It does not suddenly make you wealthy. Post-bankruptcy, i.e. post-inflation, America and other oil consuming nations will have to earn what they spend. Thus, the US dollar will need to fall to a level that is low enough such that exports of goods and services equal imports.

That will be a painfully low level. Americans were spending significantly more than they made every year from 2004 through 2007 by borrowing from abroad using their homes as collateral. This process has been continued by the Federal government's borrowing from abroad, although the magnitude of the borrowing has dropped somewhat.

Indeed, because of the recession in the US and continued growth in the developing world, trade in goods and services *excluding oil* is now almost in balance. Without oil, the monthly trade deficit is only about 15 billion dollars as of this writing in early 2010. That is less than 200 billion dollars a year and only 1.3% of GDP. Not a problem.

However, the trade deficit due solely to oil is still running at about 25 billion dollars a month with prices around $80 a barrel. When Peak Oil really hits in the years ahead and oil goes to $250-300 a barrel, the oil deficit alone will be 75 billion dollars a month.

Already anxious about the existing debt burden, foreigners are not going to be eager to lend the US an additional trillion dollars per year to buy imported oil. In the simplest terms, repaying a foreign debt requires running a trade surplus to generate cash for repayment, just as paying down a debt of your own requires earning more than you spend. How will America run trade surpluses with $300 oil? It can't.

With oil at $300, even the existing debt can realistically never be repaid. Why would foreigners wish to add to the already significant losses they will be suffering? They won't.

Realistically, the nation as a whole will have, by about 2015 or so, to reduce spending to a level it can afford given the high cost of oil. Of necessity, Americans will return to a simpler way of life.

The focus will be on generating exportable goods and services to finance the oil bill each month. We will have to run a trillion dollar per year trade surplus excluding oil to bring overall trade into balance. Currently, exports are approximately 1.8 trillion dollars a year, so this is not impossible.

One way this can happen is by having massive unemployment in those sectors of the economy that do not generate exportable goods and services, such as residential construction and real estate. Unemployed people use less gasoline and buy less stuff at Wal-Mart. Trade *will* ultimately balance.

The fact is that we can get by on a lot less than we have been. And in the future, we will need to. Our adaptation to this "lower standard of living" will inevitably be viewed as the Second Great Depression, as the economy contracts in real terms by 15%-25% from 2007 levels.

CHAPTER 6

A Probable Timeline for the Second Great Depression

Peak Oil is an event the consequences of which will play out over decades not years. The Second Great Depression will occur over roughly twenty years and will be comprised of three main phases: 1. Asset Deflation (2008-2012), 2. Inflation (2013-2020), and 3. Hyperinflation (2021-2029).

We are currently in the first phase, Asset Deflation. Consumer prices are fairly stable. The official consumer price index is showing inflation running at around 2%. Falling rents as a result of the collapse of the housing bubble is helping keep inflation down as rent comprises around 40% of the CPI.

Alternate measures of inflation that avoid the nonsensical adjustments made by the government's statisticians to try to make politicians look good are running at around 5%.

Asset prices, however, are falling dramatically. The stock market is off significantly even after the recent bull market advance. Home prices have fallen 50% in some areas and very significantly almost everywhere else. Commercial real estate, corporate bonds, you name it, prices have dropped dramatically.

Only Treasury securities have performed well.

This Asset Deflation phase of the Second Great Depression will last until about 2012. Essentially, all the money printing that the Federal Reserve is currently doing is just offsetting the deflationary forces that are at work as a result of the contraction of credit in the private economy.

The Fed only controls the base money supply. The "money multiplier" that further increases the overall supply of money in the economy is controlled by private lending. For insight into how private bankers "print money" see Peter Bernstein's *A Primer on Money, Banking and Gold*. It is the best and easiest to understand explanation I have ever read on this quite mysterious subject.

Recently, private lending has been dramatically curtailed as lenders find few individuals capable of taking on more debt. In the first quarter of 2010, over 95% of all new mortgages were issued by the government-sponsored entities Fannie Mae, Freddie Mac and Ginnie Mae. Most large banks are terrified to make new loans and increase their already massive exposure to potential defaults.

Individuals themselves are likewise reluctant to borrow further and are indeed seeking to pay down the debt they have. The era of truly reckless lending and borrowing is clearly over. Every foreclosure that occurs reduces the money multiplier further by taking another private loan out of existence.

Many foreclosures are resold at far lower prices (often to investors paying cash) with a great reduction in net borrowing. The effect of this collapse of private lending is deflationary since it reduces the overall supply of money in the economy.

The purchase of over a trillion dollars of assets by the Federal Reserve has thus far only stabilized consumer prices. Banks are hoarding cash, bracing for the next decline in real estate prices and the next wave of defaults. Asset prices continue to fall back to more reasonable levels.

What we are experiencing is the Asset Deflation phase of the Second Great Depression.

Phase two of the Second Great Depression will be the Inflation phase. This phase will last from approximately 2013 through 2020. Once asset prices are stabilized, at low levels, and once the deflationary impact of the reduction of the money multiplier effect due to the contraction of private lending has run its course as the second wave of foreclosures comes to an end, there will be nothing to offset the inflationary impact of continued deficit spending together with continued Federal Reserve monetization of the resulting governmental borrowing.

Likewise, the period 2011-2014 will see the next wave of the oil shock as the surplus capacity created by the economic collapse of 2007-09 is absorbed by continued growth in the developing world, increased consumption in the oil exporting nations and by continued production declines in existing fields.

Typically, inflationary processes start gradually. We can expect significant continued budget deficits as America deals with an overextended military, out of control entitlement programs running cash flow deficits, together with the ongoing attempts of policy makers to offset the deleterious economic effects of $8.00 gasoline, i.e. more "cash for clunkers" type programs. Economic contraction will limit tax revenues as businesses struggle to make a profit and individuals remain out of work.

Finally, in phase three, Hyperinflation, the federal government will abandon its attempt to manage the fiscal and economic crisis in an even remotely responsible manner. In the period 2021-2030, economic stimulus, an overstretched US military, social welfare including health care for all Americans, together with the Social Security and Medicare programs (now dramatically in deficit and adding significantly to the overall debt burden) will overwhelm the government's ability to secure resources.

Oil prices will have surged to $300 per barrel (in 2010 dollars) to create tremendous strain on public resources as the level of unemployment reaches levels only before seen in this country during the First Great Depression. Real unemployment will reach

35%, while even government statistics will reflect a 20% unemployment rate.

Necessarily, the precise timing of these events is uncertain at this point. But the basic timeline will prove true: inflation picking up somewhere around 2013 and then accelerating dramatically a decade or so later to hyperinflation in the economic chaos caused by $300 oil.

By hyperinflation, I mean any rate of inflation over 20% per year. A German 1920's style inflation of thousands of percent per year (as was recently seen in Zimbabwe) is not necessary or likely. As long as Americans are willing to pay some taxes, budget deficits will not reach levels large enough to require that level of money printing.

However, a significant reduction in (or virtual elimination of) debt levels will be needed, and for that purpose a 5-10 fold increase in the price level can reasonably be expected. This can be achieved by averaging 10-15% inflation for the entire period 2013 to 2030.

Part Two:
An Investing Strategy for a Post-Peak World

CHAPTER 7

Investing, 2010 Through 2030

Investing successfully is usually about getting the big-picture trends right and staying in for the long haul. Long-term bonds generated miserable returns during the inflation between 1964 and 1982. Since then, they have performed very well during the disinflation of 1982 through 2008.

In real terms, the stock market declined 75% between 1968 and 1982, a crash that in inflation-adjusted terms rivaled that of the First Great Depression. Stocks thereafter rose more than 10-fold between 1982 and 2000, with the Dow rising from around 1,000 to over 10,000, while inflation remained relatively low.

The key is to find the inflection point and get the long-term trend right. Based on long-term measures of value, such as price relative to ten year average earnings, stocks are once again overvalued (as of this writing in early 2010). We are likely, given the turbulence ahead, to see another brutal bear market in coming years, perhaps several. Stocks will once again sell at historically low ten year average earnings multiples, somewhere in the single digits.

The one thing that can be said for Great Depressions is that they do offer excellent opportunities for purchasing equities at bargain prices. Expect the next bear market to begin shortly after the next big spike in oil prices in 2011-2014. A sharp rise in oil prices is actually the single best predictor of bear markets in equities. For a thorough discussion of this subject see Stephen Leeb's *The Oil Factor.*

The key going forward will be to invest in those sectors of the economy that will outperform in the decades ahead, and to avoid those that will continue to struggle. Traditional Energy, Alternative Energy, Consumer Staples, Basic Materials and Utilities stocks are most likely the sectors of the economy you will want to be invested in.

The next few years (2010-2014) very well may produce fresh lows in the stock market with the S&P 500 bottoming somewhere around 600, as real home prices continue to decline, the economy continues to shed jobs and oil prices rocket up to painfully high levels. This book is not about market-timing, however. I recommend that you disregard the value of the market indexes (such as the Dow Jones Industrial Average or S&P 500) and instead focus on allocation between asset classes and sector weighting.

Furthermore, with all the money being created at the present time and the wave of inflation that is coming, being out of stocks and invested in cash or bonds will be a very big mistake over the next two decades.

CHAPTER **8**

Sector Selections

For most investors, the following allocation for equities will be ideal: 20% traditional energy, 20% alternative energy (including nuclear), 20% consumer staples, 20% basic materials and 20% utilities. The goal is to provide enough diversification for sound investing given the uncertainty of the future and yet to focus on those sectors of the economy that will perform the best during the coming turmoil.

Excluded from the list are the following sectors, which should generally should be avoided: consumer discretionary, financials, health care, industrials and technology.

I recommend investing through sector ETF's. These provide a very low-cost way to gain diversification in those sectors of the economy that will outperform Post-Peak. Most of the ETF's discussed below simply track indexes that comprise sectors within the S&P 500. They can be purchased through any brokerage account.

TRADITIONAL ENERGY

While 20% might seem like a lot to invest in traditional energy, at the end of the surge in oil prices in the 1970's, energy companies represented 25% of the S&P 500. By 2000, at the height of the tech bubble, they had fallen to just 3%. Which do you think is a more accurate representation of the value of oil, natural gas and coal to the overall economy?

Obviously, one should be concerned about the nationalization of the major oil companies or high windfall profits taxes Post-Peak. But the traditional energy sector is large, including not just oil, but also natural gas and coal. While Exxon-Mobil, Chevron-Texaco and a few other very large oil companies might be effectively nationalized post-Peak, there will likely be compensation to shareholders if that occurs. There are also many other players, including exploration and production companies and oil service companies, that will survive to generate astonishing returns.

A diversified investment in the oil and gas industry is simple: an ETF such as XLE provides exposure to the entire field. I place 20% of equities in the Peak Oil Portfolio in XLE.

Alternative Energy

I allocate 20% to alternative energy as well. That might seem like a lot. However, our civilization is about to undergo a fundamental transformation from relying on fossil fuels to generating energy from alternative sources (including nuclear.)

Thus, looking forward, rather than backward, one will want to be invested in the sectors that will dominate our economy in the decades ahead. This includes nuclear for the simple reason that solar and wind power are unlikely to generate any significant percentage of our total energy usage any time soon.

In order to diversify within alternative energy, I recommend a 10% allocation to the nuclear energy ETF, PKN, which holds a wide variety of nuclear energy industry companies, and a 10% allocation to alternative energy ETF Wilderhill Clean Energy, PBW, which holds a wide variety of companies involved in solar and wind energy production.

The allocations recommended seem to focus on small sectors of the economy. In actuality, they simply focus on the real economy, not the make-believe economy of 2002 to 2008 that involved simply moving money from one person to another and charging a fee for doing so.

CONSUMER STAPLES

The Peak Oil Portfolio allocates 20% to consumer staples. The idea behind this is that people are not going to stop eating, drinking, smoking, or washing their clothes, no matter how bad things get. Indeed, studies have shown that slow-growing consumer staples companies outperform other stocks over the long-term, even during good times. This is largely because investors fail to appreciate the power of reinvested dividends for generating a high total return.

Indeed, the single best performing stock over the course of the 20th Century on a total return basis (i.e. including reinvested dividends) was not IBM or DuPont. It was Phillip Morris. When the price at the pump hits $8.00, people may not buy a new house; they may not buy new furniture or a new car, they may not go to Disneyland, but they will spend money on everyday items, including cigarettes.

The companies in the consumer staples sector will outperform the rest of the market as a result. Procter and Gamble, Walmart, Kraft, Colgate, and Coca-Cola are just a few of the names in the consumer staples ETF that trades under the ticker symbol XLP. XLP also offers a dividend yield of around 3% at current prices.

MATERIALS

Basic materials companies tend to do well in an inflationary environment. Add in a commodities boom that is likely to last several decades, and the materials sector is very likely to outperform the market for the foreseeable future. The sector ETF that trades under the ticker symbol XLB holds such companies as DuPont, Dow, Alcoa, Newmont Mining, Montsanto and Freeport McMoran.

Our planet cannot sustain a limitless number of people consuming like Americans. Ultimately, the demands of an industrializing China and India will put enormous pressure on the supply of basic materials such as oil, natural gas, coal, base metals, grains, etc.

In addition, the destruction of the value of our paper money will make gold reappear as a store of value. This will create a boom in gold mining shares such as Newmont Mining.

The Peak Oil Portfolio places 20% in materials stocks under the ticker symbol XLB. These stocks also yield around 3% in dividend income at the time of this writing in early-2010.

UTILITIES

One of the keys to investing in any market, but especially during difficult times is to focus on dividends. Investors tend to get distracted by price fluctuations. It is commonly stated that US stock prices did not return to their 1929 peak level until November 1958. This fact, while technically accurate, completely misstates the actual performance of equity investments over that time.

Dividends matter. Including dividends, an investment in common stocks regained its 1929 value (in inflation-adjusted terms) briefly in 1937, and again permanently in 1944 after a wait of 15 years. By 1958, the total return of the stock market was up nearly 400%. Of course, 1929 was the height of a fantastic bubble and a terrible time to move from cash into stocks. The First Great Depression and WWII didn't help things much.

However, investors who accumulated shares gradually over the course of the 1920's and 1930's and who avoided leverage, were able to acquire a large portion of their shares at the bargain prices of the early 1920's and during the depths of the First Great Depression.

Investors can accumulate shares in companies in the sectors recommended in this book in two ways: 1) by saving from outside income and 2) by reinvesting dividends. Prolonged bear markets are actually great opportunities to accumulate shares both by addition to positions with new money and by reinvesting dividends.

Utility stocks, which typically pay very healthy dividends, comprise 20% of the equities in the Peak Oil Portfolio. Utilities can be purchased via the ETF that trades under the ticker symbol XLU. Underlying companies include Exelon, FPL, Dominion Resources, Southern Co. and Duke Energy.

The dividend yield on the XLU as of this writing is around 5%. There are certainly challenges for the utility industry going forward including restrictions on coal use due to environmental concerns.

Even when times are tough, however, people still need electricity. The transition to wind, solar and nuclear will, if anything, justify further cost increases to consumers.

CHAPTER 9

Sectors to Avoid

Not listed above are five significant S&P sectors: consumer discretionary, financials, health care, industrials and technology. Here is why I exclude these sectors from the Peak Oil Portfolio.

Consumer Discretionary

Consumer discretionary will be a loser for the simple reason that consumers just aren't going to have much discretionary income. Simpler times are coming to America. Peak Oil, together with a newfound fear of debt as a result of the crash of the real estate bubble, is going to return Americans to simpler tastes and a focus on needs versus wants. In general, this won't be good for big box retailers, cable companies, fast food chains, theme park operators and other companies in the consumer discretionary sector.

When gas is $8.00 a gallon, the focus will be on putting food on the table. Far fewer families will be shelling out $200 to go to Disneyland or will be able to pay $100 for cable television every month.

FINANCIALS

Financial stocks should be avoided more than any other sector of the economy in the decades ahead. Americans are undergoing a fundamental transformation in how they view debt. During the period from 2002 to 2008, the sector of the economy that involved moving money from one person to another boomed as consumer debt reached levels never before seen in American history, indeed world history.

Much of that debt will never be repaid. The largest banks in the nation became insolvent as a result of the real estate crash and the many reckless loans that were made against insufficient reserves. They have survived only as a result of the trillions of dollars that have been given to them by both Congress and the Fed in exchange for their toxic loans and through the assumption of the obligations, i.e. the "losing bets" of failed institutions such as AIG and Bear Stearns. Banks are also being aided by the maintenance of short-term interest rates (at which banks borrow from the Fed and pay you and me on deposits) at near zero levels.

The financial sector is in for a very rough period ahead as we transition to a brave new world in which people first earn money, then spend it. While inflation will certainly create opportunities for speculation and healthy profits for some on Wall Street, as a percentage of the total economy, finance will shrink dramatically as American attitudes toward debt change.

HEALTHCARE

Another sector to avoid Post-Peak is healthcare. Americans spend an inordinate amount of money on healthcare compared to other advanced nations. Post-Peak, a lot of fat will be cut out of the economy. Healthcare offers a lot of fat for the cutting.

The big drug and biotech companies that comprise the healthcare sector are unlikely to perform well, despite an aging population. Ultimately, nationalization of the healthcare system is likely coming in one form or another and this will *not* be good for healthcare stocks.

Americans are demanding cheaper healthcare, and they are going to get it. Eventually.

INDUSTRIALS

Industrial stocks, likewise, should be avoided in the decades that follow. While scarcity of key resources such as oil probably means increased military conflict and increased military spending which will benefit some industrial companies, other industrial segment companies will struggle as the economy shrinks. These include railroads and shipping companies that will not be transporting goods that consumers and businesses are not buying.

TECHNOLOGY

Finally, technology stocks will underperform Post-Peak. When the choice is between putting food on the table (or gas in the tank) and upgrading to a faster micro-processor and larger disk drive, consumers will opt for the former. Realistically, the life of a PC can be stretched out many more years than has been common during the technology boom.

Wireless telephones and cell-phone usage also can and will be cut back on during hard times. How many families have $150 cell phone bills that they just aren't going to be able to afford with gas at $8.00 a gallon?

Part Three:
Looking Beyond the Stock Market

CHAPTER 10

Diversification Between Asset Classes

Given the difficulties that the economy is likely to face in the years ahead, The Peak Oil Portfolio does not allocate 100% to common stocks. Rather, the hedge against prolonged equity bear markets traditionally offered by bonds is replaced by an allocation of 30% of the Portfolio to direct investments in oil, silver and gold.

Thus, the complete Peak Oil Portfolio looks like this:

Consumer Staples (XLP) 14%
Traditional Energy (XLE) 14%
Alternative Energy (PBW + PKN) 14%
Materials (XLB) 14%
Utilities (XLU) 14%

Crude Oil (USL) 15%
Gold (GLD + metal) 10%
Silver (SLV + metal) 5%

CHAPTER 11

Crude Oil

Naturally, given the price appreciation that can be expected for crude oil, direct investments in oil futures will be good investments Post-Peak. For virtually all investors, however, futures contracts are an unsuitable investment vehicle due to the excessive leverage involved.

Fortunately, there are now exchange-traded funds (ETF's) that track the price of crude oil directly. The most popular is USO, which tracks the price of crude oil to be delivered within the next calendar month. The Peak Oil Portfolio includes an investment in a different ETF to invest in oil which trades under the ticker symbol USL.

USL holds equal investments in oil for delivery in each of the following 12 calendar months. This means that USL has lower trading costs than USO and other similar "front-month" ETF's which must roll over their inventory every month. It is just more efficient to buy oil for delivery one year from now and then sell the contract when it gets close to delivery rather than repeating the same process each month.

Should an even longer-term oil ETF begin to trade on the market, the Peak Oil Portfolio will hold its oil allocation in that form. Currently, I recommend 15% allocation to USL.

Rather than acknowledge that we are at Peak Oil and that a radical change in consumer behavior is necessary, many politicians have blamed oil speculators for high oil prices. This is foolishness, as no speculator can push up the price of oil if Saudi Arabia has sufficient oil to sell at a lower price.

We can expect, however, continued regulation of the futures markets, especially in oil. Already one leveraged oil ETF has had to close down (DXO). Should all oil ETF's be shut down, which is not at all unlikely given the magnitude of the crisis ahead, the 15% of the portfolio devoted to crude oil via USL will be replaced with the equities most closely tied to the price of crude oil, the oil and gas exploration and production stocks. These can be purchased under the ticker symbol XOP.

CHAPTER **12**

Gold and Silver

For 5,000 years, gold has been money. It was in this country as well until 1933 when, in the depths of the First Great Depression, Franklin Roosevelt suspended the convertibility of United States dollars into gold and ordered Americans to surrender most of their gold to the government.

FDR gave an American about $20 in paper money for an ounce of gold in 1933. A piece of paper with a picture of Andrew Jackson on it is still worth twenty dollars. But an ounce of gold is now worth over $1,000, a 50-fold rise.

Gold has traditionally been valued as money for several good reasons. The most important reason is that gold can't be created at will by a government in need of funds. In the 76 years since the dollar lost its direct tie to gold, it has lost 98% of its purchasing power. That is over 4% per year, year after year after year.

When paper money starts losing its value in the Second Great Depression that we have just entered, people will look for a store of value. They will turn to gold and gold's more affordable sibling, silver.

Consequently, the Peak Oil Portfolio allocates 10% to gold. I would suggest that half of this be held in a liquid form such as the

ETF that trades under the ticker symbol GLD. The remaining half should be held in the form of physical metal such as Krugerands or gold bars.

Silver largely lost its status as money in recent decades. As this status and the corresponding "monetary premium" is regained in the decades ahead, silver should appreciate rapidly. Silver has one additional advantage over gold in being much less expensive to purchase.

Many people will wish to preserve purchasing power in the years ahead but will be unable to spend over $1,000 for a gold coin. A silver coin can be purchased for just 15 or 20 dollars of today's paper money. Increasingly, silver will be viewed as an affordable store of value and a good investment.

The Peak Oil Portfolio includes 5% allocated to silver to be held half in SLV, an ETF that tracks the price of silver, and half in physical metal. One way to buy physical silver is by purchasing Peace Silver Dollars. These were minted in the US between 1921 and 1935 and can be found on EBAY or at your neighborhood coin dealer, if your town still has one of these.

In the coming Inflationary Depression, gold will rise to $5,000 an ounce or higher. Five thousand dollars may seem like a lot now. However, in the 1970's gold rose from $35 an ounce to as high as $850, or more than 20-fold. If the Inflation of the Second Great Depression is more severe than that of the 1970's, as seems likely to be the case, then the rise in gold would be at least as great.

This would put gold in the $5,000 range up from its lows around $250 an ounce around 2000. There is a lot of paper wealth that will be seeking a safe haven in the years ahead. This could drive gold to levels that would not seem reasonable to contemplate at present.

Silver traditionally has traded at a ratio of approximately 15 to 1 with gold. Should silver regain its monetary premium, it may rise to the approximately $300 level as the traditional relationship with gold is re-established. Silver currently can be purchased for about $15.00 an ounce.

CHAPTER 13

Bonds

In the Second Great Depression, bonds will be *very* bad investments. Here's why. Even very short-term bonds will produce significantly negative returns, year after year, as the interest earned falls short of the inflation of prices. Taxes on interest income further reduce the return. As a bond-holder you are a creditor, and one of the fundamental purposes of the coming Great Inflation is to take wealth away from you and give it to some poor debtor, including perhaps the US Government, who needs it more than you do.

Thirty year government bonds are currently yielding just 4.5%. That is less than the present rate of inflation calculated using pre-Clinton era methods. (See www.shadowstats.com for more information on what current government statistics would be if calculated using the previously accepted methods.)

If you buy a 30 year bond today at 4.5%, your after tax yield might be around 3%. Should inflation average 15% over the next 20 years, your after tax real annual return would be a negative 12%. Keep that up for 20 years and you will lose over 90% of your investment. Ouch!

Even Treasury Inflation-Protected Bonds (or TIPS as they are called) are unlikely to be great investments, as TIPS are adjusted for inflation by the CPI which will likely understate inflation going forward. Why?

The government has too many benefits and payments indexed to the CPI, including Social Security benefits, retirement benefits, and TIPS themselves, to have any incentive to calculate the number correctly. Year after year we have absurd adjustments to the CPI (hedonic, geometric, etc.) so that it now bears an only distant relation to the actual increase in the cost of living.

So, if you must buy bonds, buy TIPS. But otherwise steer clear of what will likely be one of the easiest ways to lose money in the coming two decades.

CHAPTER 14

Savings Accounts and CD's

When you put cash in the bank, what you are actually doing is lending money to the bank which will pay you interest on your loan. Repayment of your loan is guaranteed up to $250,000 by the FDIC (in the US). Furthermore, the rate of interest you receive is tied closely to the short-term interest rates and these rates are largely set by the Federal Reserve.

When the Fed prints money, it doesn't normally buy beanie babies or even mortgage-backed securities. Rather, it buys Treasury securities. When it does this, the Fed drives up the price of the securities which forces yields or interest rates down. To over-simplify a little, a security yielding 2% at current prices might yield closer to 1% if its price doubles due to Fed buying.

Since the interest you earn on bank deposits is closely related to the next safest thing you can do with your money, i.e. own short-term Treasury bills, the Fed's purchase of these instruments serves to reduce the interest income on your bank deposits.

In the years ahead, in order to stimulate the economy, the rate of interest on bank deposits will be less than the rate of inflation, which eventually will hit double digits. Furthermore, interest on your deposits is taxable.

This means that it is entirely possible that in the Second Great Depression, "money in the bank" might earn 10%, while inflation is running at 15%. Taxes on the 10% might reduce your return to 7%, which would result in a return of negative 8% per year. Keep that up for twenty years and the real purchasing power of your savings will have decreased by more than 80%.

CHAPTER 15

Real Estate

Real estate "investing" was all the rage during the 1997 to 2006 boom that saw home prices double and even triple in many parts of the country. This reached a completely manic stage in 2005-06, when many homeowners in the bubble states of California, Nevada, Arizona and Florida suddenly found themselves apparently richer by anywhere from $100,000 to a million dollars.

Modest middle class homes in neighborhoods in Southern California, where I live, sold for over a million dollars each. Yet despite the record increases in home prices, household equity fell to historic lows as cash-out financing sucked equity out of homes faster than it was accumulating via price appreciation.

Wages, by contrast, barely budged during this time. The manic stage of the bubble was supported by financing that can only be described as completely insane. Exploding mortgages with teaser rates as well as negatively amortizing loans were all too common as buyers struggled to get in on the action.

At the very height, a strawberry picker in Ventura County, California was reportedly given a $750,000 loan to buy a house, despite the fact that he earned little more than the state's minimum hourly wage of $7.50. All too predictably, the bubble popped and home prices began to fall. Now, in many areas, homes are already back to their 2001 prices.

What all these real estate "investors" did not, apparently, realize is that the long term return on residential real estate is zero. Real estate is a consumption item. It provides value to the owner by serving as a place to live.

It is only *inflation* that creates the illusion that one's home is an investment. Houses seem to go up 4% in value, year after year, when in actuality it is only the value of paper money that is declining. Expressed in terms of barrels of oil, loaves of bread, teachers' salaries and cowboy boots, home prices are the same now as they were 100 years ago. Indeed, without constant repairs, a home's real value actually declines.

While a dwelling itself will not normally appreciate in value in real terms, owning a home does allow households to save in a tax advantaged manner. Since mortgage interest is deductible for most homeowners, the costs of borrowing to purchase a home is deductible currently, while the price appreciation is tax-deferred or escapes tax entirely. The financial benefit of owning a home as opposed to renting is almost entirely found in its tax treatment.

In areas that were hit hard by the first wave of foreclosures, homes are now selling for significantly less than the cost of construction. These would be very good investments at the present time as builders will not resume building in these areas until they can at least break even. A return to construction cost can reasonably be expected within the decade.

In other areas, however, housing remains problematic as prices are still unaffordable with traditional financing and many homes are waiting to be sold in the coming second wave of foreclosures. Furthermore, underwater homeowners will need to walk away if they have to relocate or lose their job.

Finally, in what will be the greatest blow to the housing market in the years ahead, interest rates will rise with inflation. Much of the appreciation in housing from 1997 to 2006, was due to continuously falling interest rates that allowed individuals to afford the monthly payment on higher and higher dollar value mortgages. This process will run in reverse as mortgage rates rise.

A return to even 9% mortgages will keep home prices from rising even as wages climb. The real value of homes will fall as their nominal prices remain unchanged despite inflation running at 10-15%.

Ultimately, however, especially beginning around 2012, homeowners who can hold on over the next two decades will find the real value of their fixed mortgage obligations dramatically reduced as the value of paper dollars and obligations tied to paper dollars diminishes rapidly.

Between 2012 and 2030, homes will actually turn out to be fantastic investments, but only to the extent they are financed by long-term mortgages at low interest rates. The real value of the homes themselves will not increase, but the real value of the mortgages attached to them will diminish significantly, creating a windfall for highly indebted homeowners. This windfall will come at the expense of both renters and those who own their homes free and clear.

The real estate boom was a product of the inflationary forces generated by the explosion of private lending due to innovations in mortgage finance. It encouraged many individuals to abandon productive careers to try to make money from what were just changes in the prices of non-productive assets.

Perhaps government should not interfere in reckless lending. After all, that is a matter between a bank and a borrower. However, the shareholders and bondholders of the reckless banks should be the ones to suffer the consequences if the reckless borrower defaults. That is what capitalism is all about. This the Fed and Congress did not allow to happen. Call it Socialism for the rich.

Inflation has many perverse effects. One of these is that those who pay down debt and save are often penalized, while those who speculate and go into debt are often rewarded. Inflation has the effect of discouraging thrift and hard work in those areas of the economy that create real wealth. It encourages everyone to become a speculator.

In the hyperinflation of the next two decades, much attention will be given to making money from mere price changes. The great casino of Wall Street, which produces nothing, will to some extent become even more influential than it is now. Indeed, if the price level rises ten-fold, the stock market should rise by roughly the same amount. That will generate a great deal of interest.

However, to the extent we focus as a nation on this ultimately non-productive activity, we will lose our competitive position in the global economy. At the same time, a rational individual cannot ignore price changes in an inflationary environment since they become so important to investment outcomes.

Part Four:
Model Portfolios

CHAPTER 16

The Peak Oil Portfolio, Retirement Edition

Readers approaching or already in retirement may be concerned about the high weighting given to equities in the Peak Oil Portfolio given the damage already suffered in the bear markets of 2000-02 and 2007-09.

However, the outperformance of the energy and materials sectors of the portfolio (60% of the total allocation to stocks) during bull market phases should more than compensate for losses in the portfolio during downturns. Furthermore, consumer discretionary and utilities stocks tend to do well during downturns on a relative basis.

Should investors wish a more conservative portfolio allocation, however, I would recommend the following.

Peak Oil Portfolio, Retirement Edition

Stocks:	40%
XLP	8%
XLE	8%
PBW + PKN	8%
XLB	8%
XLU	8%
Bonds:	40%
TIPS	40%
Commodities:	20%
USL (XOP)	10%
GLD	7%
SLV	3%

While 20% allocated to commodities may seem high for a "low risk" portfolio, there are several advantages to this allocation. First, diversification between asset classes including commodities does reduce overall risks for a portfolio as commodities are often increasing in value when stocks and bonds are falling.

Second, commodities, especially energy and precious metals, are going to be the winners in the hard times ahead. As inflation kicks in and investors flee from bonds and cash, precious metals will rise tremendously in value.

CHAPTER 17

The Peak Oil Portfolio: "Young Turk" Edition

There will be some readers, younger in age perhaps, for whom investing in utilities stocks and consumer staples seems a bit too dull. If you are in your 20's or 30's or otherwise wish to maximize the growth of your portfolio without regard to short-term ups or downs, I recommend a heavier weighting in commodities and a slightly different allocation among sectors.

Peak Oil Portfolio, "Young Turk" Edition

Stocks:	70%
Traditional Energy (XLE)	17.5%
Alternative Energy (PBW+PKN)	17.5%
Materials (XLB)	17.5%
Precious Metals (GDX)	17.5%
Commodities	30%
Crude Oil (USL or XOP)	15%
Gold (GLD)	10%
Silver (SLV)	5%

This is not a portfolio for the faint of heart. However, if we are actually past Peak Oil and looking at a hyperinflationary depression in the decades ahead, a risk tolerant investor will benefit from being invested primarily in energy and basic materials, with a heavy dose of precious metals mining shares to boot. Likewise, oil at $500 a barrel and gold at $5,000 an ounce will result in tremendous real returns for investors in the energy and precious metals ETF's.

Clearly, this strategy would not be suitable for everyone.

You can track the performance of the model portfolios recommended in this book compared to the broad market index at my website: www.peakoilportfolio.com.

CHAPTER **18**

Conclusion

Peak Oil (2005-08) marks a turning point in the history of human civilization. The turmoil caused by chronic oil shortages will coincide with the end of American hegemony and the return to a truly multi-polar world in which Europe, the US, China and Japan vie for influence and power.

I don't discuss military "solutions" to the oil supply problem in this book, but will make just one comment on this issue: there are no military solutions to Peak Oil. One of the key reasons that the Allies prevailed in World War II was that their oil supply infrastructure was located safely in North America and Western Siberia.

Germany was dependent on production in Eastern Europe which was vulnerable to bombing raids. Japan was dependent on imported oil from Indonesia which could be cut off by naval blockade. Indeed, it was the blockade of Indonesian oil imports to Japan that triggered the bombing of Pearl Harbor.

In an age of cruise missiles and ICBM's, military conflict over the fragile and explosive oil infrastructure in the Middle East and elsewhere would be most unwise for all combatant nations.

The US is the most powerful nation in the world, there is no doubt. But with just 15% of world GDP, we are in no position to maintain our current empire. What the US needs is a graceful retreat to our own hemisphere as part of the coming downsizing.

I have no doubt that this very reasonable proposal will be ignored in Washington. Only radicals such as Ron Paul (on the right) and Dennis Kucinich (on the left) support such an idea.

The Second Great Depression has already begun. Things will be difficult. I certainly hope that American politicians are wise enough to avoid making them too much more difficult than they will already be.

About the Author

Kenneth D. Worth is an attorney based in Riverside County, California. He holds a bachelor's degree from Stanford University, a master's degree from the Claremont Graduate School and a *juris doctor degree* from the University of California at Los Angeles (UCLA).

9 781432 760847